Table of Contents

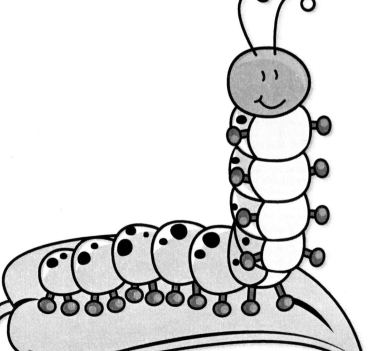

Counting to the 100th Day of School

For younger children counting toward a 100th day of school celebration can be fun and exciting. As part of the class daily routine or calendar time, incorporate counting the number of days in school. By counting to 100 using a variety of methods, students will have consistent opportunities to reinforce important counting and place value concepts. Place value is a keystone math concept providing the foundation for learning to add and subtract double digit numbers.

Here are some activities for counting towards the 100th day of school.

Create a Number Line:

Note each day of school by displaying the number. Perhaps create a hundred chart or display the numbers above the chalkboard to make a number line around the classroom. Encourage students to estimate where the 100th day mark will be in the classroom.

For Example:

Number Of Days	1	2	3	4	5	6	7	etc.

Trade Up To 100 Using Coins

Trading up to 100 using coins is an excellent way to introduce coin values and to review them in a meaningful way. On the first day, start with a penny, then add a penny each subsequent day until the fifth day. Then trade up to a nickel. After 10 days, trade up to dime, then to a quarter etc, until the class reaches a loonie to represent the 100th day. Place magnetic strips on the back of real coins and display them on the chalkboard.

Bundle Popsicle Sticks Or Straws

Help students understand the concept of the 1's, 10's and 100's place by bundling popsicle sticks or straws to represent each place value. Set up three empty cans and label them, 1's, 10's and 100's. Each day add a popsicle stick or straw to the 1's can. Once you reach ten, bundle the popsicle sticks or straws and place the "10's bundle" to demonstrate one group of ten in the 10's can. For example, for day 36, there would be six popsicle sticks or straws in the 1's can and three "10's" bundles of popsicle sticks or straws in the 10's can.

100 Chart

On a 100 chart, practice skip counting to 100 by 1's, 2's, 5's and 10's. Challenge students to find numbers on the 100 chart using math language. For example, find all the numbers with the number 8 in the ones place.

Tally Chart

Keep a running tally on the chalkboard of how many days you have been in school. In addition, the teacher may wish to challenge students to predict the date of the 100th day of school.

Chalkboard Publishing © 2007

100th Day Celebration!

Dear Parents and Guardians,

On _____ it will be the 100th day of school. Our class will be celebrating by participating in different activities throughout the day.

As part of the celebration children are asked to bring a "100" collection from home to share with their classmates. For example: 100 jelly beans, 100 buttons, 100 paper clips, 100 stamps, or 100 stickers. Children are encouraged to arrange their collections in groups of 2, 5, 10, etc. Some suggestions to display your child's 100 collection include:

- poster board
- shoebox
- container
- jar
- boxr
- folder
- plastic baggie
- backpack

As part of the 100 theme, we are also asking students to dress up as if they are 100 years old. In addition, if you have a family member who is 100 years old, who would be willing and able to visit the class, please let us know!

Your family's participation is greatly appreciated!

Kind regards,

_____

3

LET'S GIVE A CHEER
100TH DAY IS HERE!

WE'VE LEARNED A LOT ALONG THE WAY!
TIME TO CELEBRATE OUR 100TH DAY!

HIP! HIP! HOORAY!

WE HAVE BEEN IN SCHOOL
FOR 100 DAYS
LOOK AT ALL
WE LEARNED
ALONG THE WAY!

HOORAY! HOORAY! IT'S 100 DAY!
COUNT TO 100 IN DIFFERENT WAYS!

COUNT BY 1'S - IT'S REALLY FUN!
1, 2, 3, 4, 5, ...

COUNT BY 2'S - I WILL COUNT WITH YOU!
2, 4, 6, 8, 10, ...

COUNT BY 5'S - IT'S EASY IF YOU TRY!
5, 10, 15, 20, 25, ...

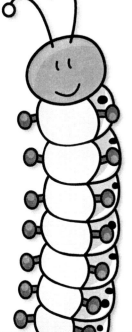

COUNT BY 10'S
AND THEN
START OVER AGAIN!
10, 20, 30, 40, ...

100th Day of School Activity Cards

The 100th Day Activity Cards are intended to be used with a whole group, small group, or as independent Celebration Stations. At the end of this teacher resource book are blank line masters that work with some of the cards.

Whole Group Ideas

- As a class, participate in 100 second physical activity challenges. Give each child a recording sheet to record their results.

- As a class effort, complete the activity cards that must list or name 100 things. For instance name 100 Canadian animals, list 100 questions, etc.

- As a class, stay silent for 100 seconds.

- The teacher may wish to send the cards home as family challenges.

Celebration Stations

Use the 100th Day Activity Cards as celebration stations. Students will enjoy interacting and completing the cards on their own, or with their peers.

Teacher Tips:

1. Choose the time block that best suits the class schedule. If possible, have children participate in a variety of 100th Day Celebration Activity Stations.

2. Decide how many Celebration Stations will be set up and what they will be. The teacher may wish to balance the activities so that some activities need minimum teacher direction with some that require more teacher guidance.

3. Store what is needed for each chosen activity in a bin, so that it is organized and ready to go. The teacher may wish to include a sample of completed work to show students.

4. Before beginning, introduce and explain the expectations of each 100th Day Celebration Station. This is the time to teach any specific skills needed to complete an activity.

5. Review the number of students allowed at each Celebration Station, along with behaviour expectations.

String a necklace with 100 pieces of a cereal!

How many jumping jacks can you do in 100 seconds?

Guess how far 100 steps will take you!

Bounce a ball 100 times.

Jog on the spot for 100 seconds.

How many times can you bounce a ball in 100 seconds?

Dance the twist for 100 seconds.

How many times can you skip rope in 100 seconds?

How many times can you hula hoop in 100 seconds?

How many sit-ups can you do in 100 seconds?

How many times can you touch your head, knees and toes in 100 seconds?

Be silent for 100 seconds.

What is the length of 100 pennies?

How many push-ups can you do in 100 seconds?

What is the weight of 100 pennies?

Solve a puzzle with 100 pieces.

Print 100 words.

Write a journal:

Write about what you think it would be like to be 100 years old.

100th Day of School Activity Cards

Create a 100th day stamp.

Write a 100th day postcard.

Draw a portrait of yourself on your 100th birthday.

Draw a picture of what the world will look like in 100 years.

Draw a picture of what the world looked like 100 years ago.

Create an advertisement poster for 100th day.

Count to 100
by 1's.

Count to 100
by 2's.

Count to 100
by 5's.

Count to 100
by 10's.

How many ways
can you make
a $1.00 using
different coins?

How many ways
can you make
$100.00 using bills
and coins?

100th Day of School Activity Cards

Count backward
by 1's from 100.

Count backward
by 2's from 100.

Count backward
by 5's from 100.

Count backward
by 10's from 100.

Count backward
by 25's from 100.

Count to 100
by 25's.

100th Day of School Activity Cards

Make a picture using 100 pieces of macaroni.

Build a structure using 100 blocks.

Build a structure 100 cm high.

Create a picture using 100 shapes.

Collect 100 signatures.

Make a list of 100 of your favourite things.

What is the length of 100 nickels?

Draw a polygon with the perimeter of 100 cm.

What is the length of 100 paper clips?

Draw a polygon with the area of 100 cm².

Write 100 different numbers that are more than 100.

How much do 100 jelly beans weigh?

Make a 100th day bookmark.

What is the length of 100 crayons?

Find on a map and name communities that are 100 km away.

Measure how much water there is if you melt 100 ice cubes.

There are 7 dog years to 1 human year. If you are 100 years old, how old are you in dog years?

Flip a coin 100 times. Tally the results.

How much do 100 nickels weigh?

How much do 100 kernels of popcorn weigh?

How much do 100 paperclips weigh?

How much does 100 ml of water weigh?

Find something that measures 100 cm.

Find something that measures less than 100 cm.

Find something that measures more than 100 cm.

As a class read 100 books.

Make a colour pattern 100 cubes long.

Make a class "100 collage" with groups of 100 things.

As a class collect and donate 100 cans of food.

Count to 100 by 4's.

Can you hold your breath for 100 seconds?

Can you hum for 100 seconds?

Can you laugh for 100 seconds?

Can you balance on 1 foot for 100 seconds?

Can you stand frozen like a statue for 100 seconds?

How many times can you blink your eyes in 100 seconds?

As a class make a list of 100 adjectives.

As a class make a list of 100 verbs.

As a class make a list of 100 nouns.

As a class make a list of 100 Canadian animals.

Write a journal:

What would you do if you could have 100 wishes granted?

Write a journal:

You have just won $100 dollars! How will you spend your money?

Run a 100 m dash.

Make a 100th day crown.

Make a paper chain 100 links long.

Dress up as if you are 100 years old.

Write a journal:

Would you rather eat 100 jelly beans or 100 pieces of popcorn?

Write a journal:

What do you think it would be like to have 100 pets?

Drink 100 ml of juice.

Write a journal:
I could eat 100 _____.

On what date will you be 100 years old? Explain your thinking.

Write a journal:
If I had 100 _____ I would...

Write a 100 word long story.

Research and name things that have been invented in the last 100 years.

Sing, "Happy 100th Day To Us" to the tune of "Happy Birthday."

Write a journal:

In the first 100 days of school I have learned...

How many metres is 100 km?

Write a journal:

The best part of 100th day is...

Write an acrostic poem for the word hundred.

Make a snack mix with 100 goodies.

As a class collect
100 jokes
or riddles.

Write a journal:
I have been told
100 times
to _____.

Name a creature
that has 100 legs.

Fill in a 100 chart.

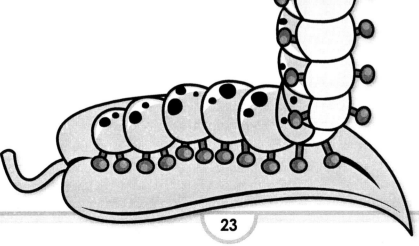

100th Day Postcard

Write a postcard to a friend about what you have learned in the first 100 days of school.

Front of Postcard:

Back of Postcard:

To:

Create a 100th day stamp.

Write about your stamp:

_____

_____

My 100th Birthday Portrait

Draw a portrait of yourself on your 100th birthday.

100th Day Advertisement Poster

Create an advertisement poster to tell people about 100th Day.
For a top quality advertisement, make sure to include:

1. A reason to celebrate 100th Day.
2. A detailed picture with neat printing.

100th Day Activity Recording Sheet

Activity	In 100 seconds, I can...

100th Day Collage

Make a 100th Day collage with 100 things.

For example: 100 stickers, 100 dots, etc.

Design a $100 Bill

Design your own Canadian $100 bill.

 **This is what a real $100 bill looks like!**

BANK OF CANADA ● BANQUE DU CANADA

100

CANADA
CENT ● ONE HUNDRED
DOLLARS

100

Write about your $100 bill:

_____

_____

Chalkboard Publishing © 2007

Design a $1.00 Coin

Design your own Canadian $1.00 coin.

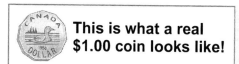 This is what a real $1.00 coin looks like!

The nickname for the Canadian $1.00 coin is the loonie. What is the nickname of your $1.00 coin and why?

_____

_____

100th Day Crown

1. Cut out a wide strip of contruction paper to fit as the band for the 100th day crown.

2. Cut out the crown below and paste it on the construction paper band.

3. Decorate your crown with 100 things.

Chalkboard Publishing © 2007

100th Day Snack Mix Recipe

Create your own 100 snack mix. Use your choice of a variety of goodies. Make sure the number of goodies add up to 100!

Number of Ingredients	What was it?

Write about your snack mix:

_____

_____

100 of Canada's Wildlife

Here are some excellent websites where you can find out more about these animals
• www.hww.ca
• www.canadianfauna.com

MAMMALS

1.	Arctic Fox	19.	Moose
2.	Atlantic walrus	20.	Mountain Goat
3.	Bats	21.	Mountain Sheep
4.	Beaver	22.	Muskox
5.	Beluga whale	23.	Muskrat
6.	Black Bear	24.	North American Bison
7.	Bowhead whale	25.	North American Elk
8.	Canada Lynx	26.	Polar Bear
9.	Caribou	27.	Porcupine
10.	Chipmunk	28.	Raccoon
11.	Cougar	29.	Red Fox
12.	Coyote	30.	Snowshoe Hare
13.	Eastern Grey Squirrel	31.	Striped Skunk
14.	Grizzly	32.	Swift Fox
15.	Harbour porpoise	33.	White-tailed Deer
16.	Killer whale	34.	Wolf
17.	Lemmings	35.	Wolverine
18.	Marten	36.	Woodchuck

AMPHIBIANS AND REPTILES

37.	Wood Frog	40.	Red-Legged Frog
38.	Leatherback Seaturtle	41.	Boreal Chorus Frog
39.	Western Garter Snake	42.	Horned Lizard

100 of Canada's Wildlife

BIRDS

43.	American Black Duck	61.	Great Blue Heron	79.	Purple Martin
44.	American Goldfinch	62.	Great Horned Owl	80.	Red-breasted Nuthatch
45.	American Robin	63.	Greater Snow Goose	81.	Redhead
46.	Arctic Tern	64.	Harlequin Duck	82.	Ring-billed Gull
47.	Atlantic Puffin	65.	Herring Gull	83.	Roseate Tern
48.	Bald Eagle	66.	Killdeer	84.	Ruby-throated Hummingbird
49.	Bicknell's Thrush	67.	Lesser Snow Goose	85.	Ruffed Grouse
50.	Black-capped Chickadee	68.	Loggerhead Shrike	86.	Seabirds
51.	Blue Jay	69.	Loons	87.	Semipalmated Sandpiper
52.	Bufflehead	70.	Mallard	88.	Sharp-shinned Hawk, Cooper's Hawk, and Northern Goshawk
53.	Burrowing Owl	71.	Marbled Murrelet	89.	Shorebirds
54.	Canada Goose	72.	Mountain Bluebird	90.	Snowy Owl
55.	Canvasback	73.	Murres	91.	Trumpeter Swan
56.	Cassin's Auklet	74.	Northern Gannet	92.	Tundra Swan
57.	Common Eider	75.	Osprey	93.	Whooping Crane
58.	Downy Woodpecker	76.	Peregrine Falcon	94.	Wild Turkey
59.	Evening Grosbeak	77.	Piping Plover	95.	Wood Duck
60.	Gray Jay	78.	Ptarmigan		

FISH

96.	Atlantic Whitefish	99.	Salmon
97.	Arctic Grayling	100.	Rainbow Trout
98.	Northern Pike		

35

Chalkboard Publishing © 2007

100th Day Bookmark

Colour in your bookmark, cut it out, fold in half and glue together!

36

Colour in the picture! Make sure to draw in tally marks on the chalkboard that add up to 100.

Celebrate the 100th Day of School!

100 Word Story

Chalkboard Publishing © 2007

You have just won $100 dollars! How will you spend your money?

What would you do if you could have
100 wishes granted? Explain your thinking.

_____

- -

_____

_____

- -

_____

_____

- -

_____

_____

_____

- -

_____

_____

What do you think it would be like to have 100 pets?

If I had **100** _____ I would...

I can eat **100** _____

100th Day acrostic Poem Fun

An acrostic poem uses the letters in a word to begin each line of the poem. Create an acrostic poem for 100th day.

H _____

U _____

N _____

D _____

R _____

E _____

D _____

100th Day Fun

45

Count to 100 Dot-to-Dot

Count by 5's to 100 and connect the dots. Colour the picture.

Brain Stretch:

Add 10 groups of 10 balloons to your picture.

Chalkboard Publishing © 2007

Count by 10's to 100 and connect the dots. Colour the picture.

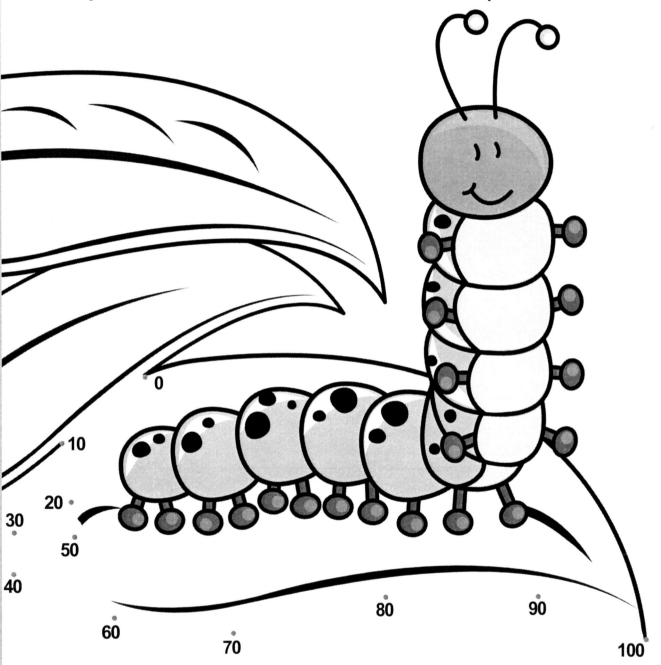

0

10

20

30

50

40

60

70

80

90

100

Brain Stretch:

Add 100 ladybugs to the picture.

100th Day Math Brain Stretch

Solve each of the problems. Show your thinking!

1. There are 7 days in a week. How many days in 100 weeks?

2. There are 12 months in a year. How many months in a 100 years?

3. There are 365 days in a year. How many days in 100 years?

100th Day Math Brain Stretch

Solve each of the problems. Show your thinking!

1. There are 60 seconds in a minute. How many seconds in 100 minutes?

2. There are 60 minutes in an hour. How many minutes in 100 hours?

49

Count and paste or draw the correct choice of coins to make $1.00.

Count and paste or draw the correct choice of bills to make $100.

100 Math Facts

1	2 + 2 =	2	9 +9=	3	8 + 6=	4	3 + 1 =
5	9 + 8=	6	5 + 1 =	7	9 + 2 =	8	7 + 6=
9	5 + 2 =	10	3 + 3 =	11	7 + 7=	12	9 + 3 =
13	8 + 6=	14	6 + 5 =	15	8 + 2 =	16	7 +1=
17	7 + 1 =	18	4 + 3 =	19	7 + 4 =	20	4 + 2 =
21	8 + 7=	22	6 + 4 =	23	0 + 1 =	24	10 + 10=
25	7 + 5 =	26	7 + 2 =	27	5 + 5 =	28	6 + 3 =
29	5 + 4 =	30	8 + 3 =	31	6 + 7=	32	6 + 1 =
33	1 + 1 =	34	10 + 6=	35	8 + 4 =	36	10 + 7=
37	10 + 1=	38	5 + 3 =	39	3 + 2 =	40	2 + 1 =
41	7 + 3 =	42	9 + 6=	43	4 + 4 =	44	6 + 6=
45	9 + 7=	46	8 + 5 =	47	8 + 1 =	48	10 + 2 =
49	4 + 1 =	50	6 + 2 =				

100 Math Facts

51	10 - 9 =	52	12 - 1 =	53	7 - 2 =	54	10 - 3 =
55	5 - 1 =	56	7 - 1 =	57	9 - 2 =	58	12 - 4 =
59	12 - 5 =	60	4 - 3 =	61	14 - 9 =	62	9 - 8 =
63	9 - 4 =	64	12 - 6 =	65	8 - 4 =	66	6 - 4 =
67	8 + 6 =	68	8 - 1 =	69	10 - 2 =	70	8 - 7 =
71	13 - 6 =	72	16 - 8 =	73	7 - 5 =	74	9 - 6 =
75	7 - 4 =	76	8 - 2 =	77	11 - 5 =	78	18 - 9 =
79	10 - 8 =	80	15 - 8 =	81	9 - 5 =	82	10 - 7 =
83	4 - 2 =	84	8 - 3 =	85	5 - 4 =	86	9 - 3 =
87	9 - 7 =	88	20 - 10 =	89	6 - 3 =	90	9 - 9 =
91	3 - 1 =	92	10 - 5 =	93	11 - 9 =	94	7 - 6 =
95	10 - 4 =	96	7 - 3 =	97	8 - 5 =	98	10 - 8 =
99	1 - 0 =	100	9 - 1 =				

100th Day Joke Fun

What do get when you cross a centipede with a parrot?

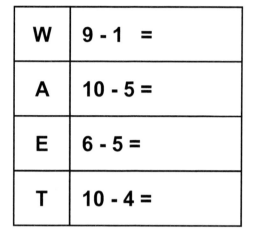

W	9 - 1 =
A	10 - 5 =
E	6 - 5 =
T	10 - 4 =

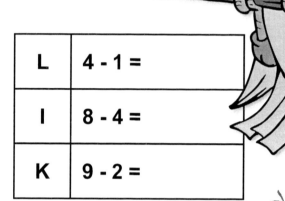

L	4 - 1 =
I	8 - 4 =
K	9 - 2 =

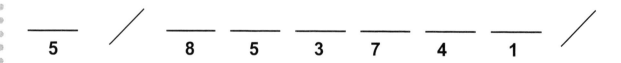

___ / ___ ___ ___ ___ ___ ___ /
5   8   5   3   7   4   1

___ ___ ___ ___ ___ ___ !
6   5   3   7   4   1

Chalkboard Publishing © 2007

What has 50 legs, but can't walk?

N	1 + 0 =
P	8 +2 =
A	2 + 2 =
T	2 + 1 =
E	4 +4 =
I	7 + 5 =

C	3 + 4 =
D	9 + 2 =
H	3 + 6 =
L	1 + 4 =
F	3 + 3 =
O	2 + 0 =

$$\underline{\hphantom{X}}_{9} \; \underline{\hphantom{X}}_{4} \; \underline{\hphantom{X}}_{5} \; \underline{\hphantom{X}}_{6} \; / \; \underline{\hphantom{X}}_{2} \; \underline{\hphantom{X}}_{6} \; / \; \underline{\hphantom{X}}_{4}$$

$$\underline{\hphantom{X}}_{7} \; \underline{\hphantom{X}}_{8} \; \underline{\hphantom{X}}_{1} \; \underline{\hphantom{X}}_{3} \; \underline{\hphantom{X}}_{12} \; \underline{\hphantom{X}}_{10} \; \underline{\hphantom{X}}_{8} \; \underline{\hphantom{X}}_{11} \; \underline{\hphantom{X}}_{8} \;!$$

First to 100!

Roll the dice! Challenge your partner to see who can reach 100 first!

What you need:

base ten pieces	a pair of dice	place value sheet

What you do:

1. Player 1 rolls the dice.

2. Player 1 counts out that number of "ones" and puts it on their place value sheet in the "ones" column.

3. Player 2 rolls the dice.

4. Player 2 counts out that number of "ones" and puts it on their place value sheet in the "ones" column.

5. Players regroup the "ones" to "tens" whenever possible.

6. The first player to regroup their "tens" to 100 wins!

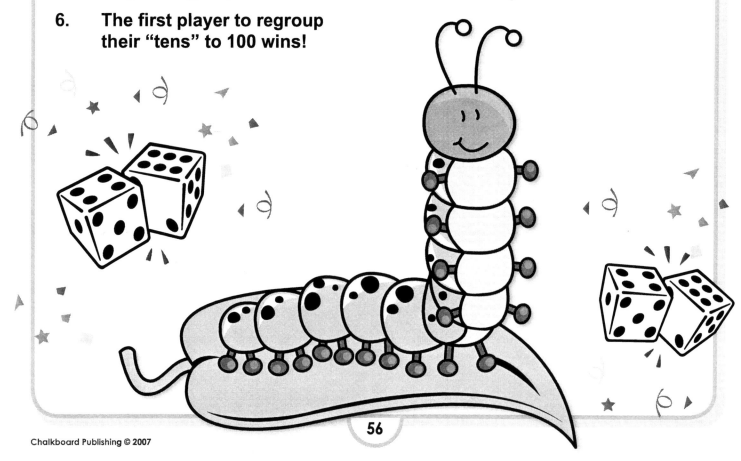

First to 100! Place Value Chart

1's	10's	100's

100th Day Math Brain Stretch

Complete the 100 chart.

1									10
							28		
31									
									60
71									
		83							
								99	

Count by 1's. Colour the number pattern in red.

Count by 2's. Colour the number pattern in blue.

Count by 5's. Mark the number pattern with green X's.

Count by 10's. Circle the numbers in orange.

Flip a coin 100 times and tally the results.

Heads	Tails

I predict that _____ will win.

After flipping a coin 100 times I found out that _____

Flip a coin 100 times and tally the results.

Heads	Tails

I predict that _____ will win.

After flipping a coin 100 times I found out that _____

100th Day Weighing Fun

How much do different collections of 100 things weigh?

100 Collection	Weight

Which collection of 100 things weighs the most?

_____

Which collection of 100 things weighs the least?

_____

CONGRATULATIONS!

You have participated in

the 100th

day

CELEBRATION!

AWARDED TO:

_____

CONGRATULATIONS!

YOU HAVE HAD

PERFECT ATTENDANCE

FOR THE FIRST

100

DAYS OF SCHOOL!

AWARDED TO:

_____

62

BOOK TITLE:

_____

READ BY:

_____

100 BOOK READ-A-THON!

100 BOOK READ -A- THON!

BOOK TITLE:

_____

READ BY:

_____

CONGRATULATIONS!

BEST DRESSED

AS A

100

YEAR OLD!

AWARDED TO:

_____

1	2	3
4	5	6
7	8	9

10	11	12
13	14	15
16	17	18

19	**20**	**21**
22	**23**	**24**
25	**26**	**27**

28	29	30
31	32	33
34	35	36

37	**38**	**39**
40	**41**	**42**
43	**44**	**45**

46	**47**	**48**
49	**50**	**51**
52	**53**	**54**

55	**56**	**57**
58	**59**	**60**
61	**62**	**63**

64	65	66
67	68	69
70	71	72

73	74	75
76	77	78
79	80	81

82	83	84
85	86	87
88	89	90

91	**92**	**93**
94	**95**	**96**
97	**98**	**99**

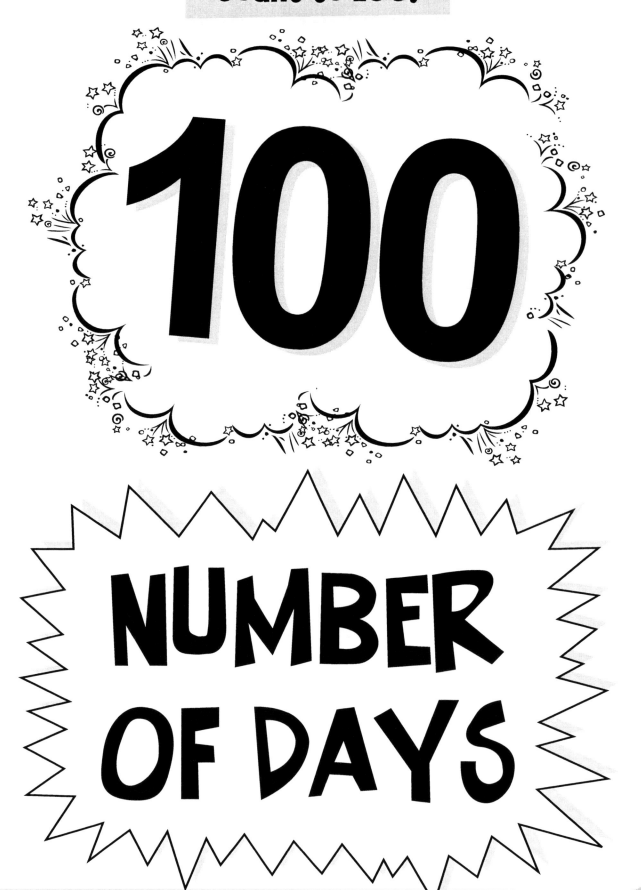

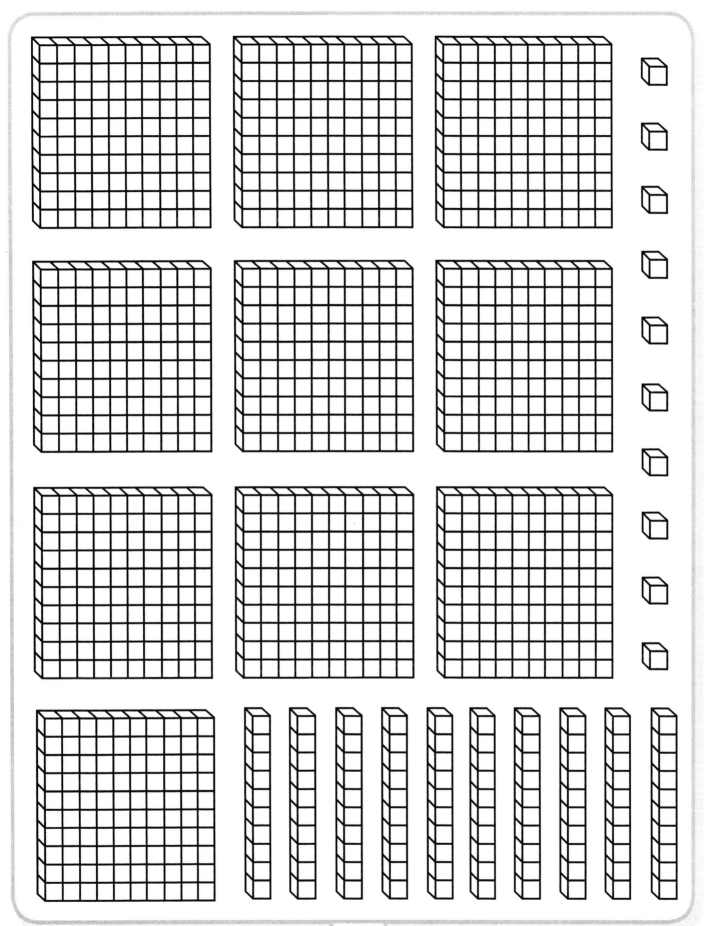

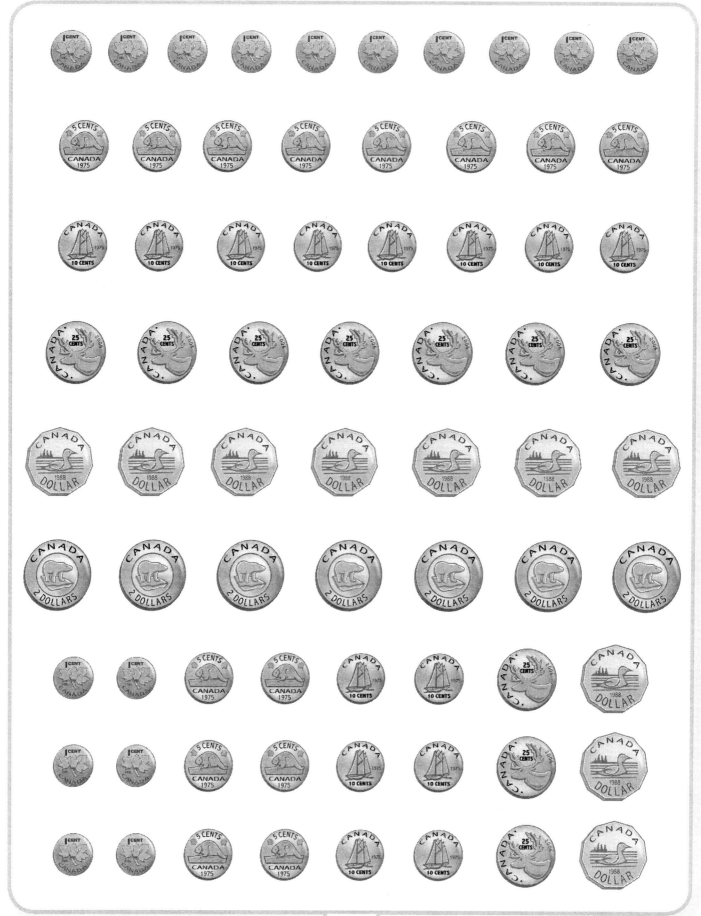

Answer Page

100th Day Math Brain Stretch, page 48

1. There are 700 days in 100 weeks.
2. There are 1200 months in 100 years.
3. There are 36 500 days in 100 years.

100th Day Math Brain Stretch, page 49

1. There are 6000 seconds in 100 minutes.
2. There are 6000 minutes in 100 hours.

Math Facts, page 64

1.	2 + 2 = 4	**26.**	7 + 2 = 9
2.	9 +9 = 18	**27.**	5 + 5 = 10
3.	8 + 6 = 14	**28.**	6 + 3 = 9
4.	3 + 1 = 4	**29.**	5 + 4 = 9
5.	9 + 8 = 17	**30.**	8 + 3 = 11
6.	5 + 1 = 6	**31.**	6 + 7 = 13
7.	9 + 2 = 11	**32.**	6 + 1 = 7
8.	7 + 6 = 13	**33.**	1 + 1 =2
9.	5 + 2 = 7	**34.**	10 + 6 = 16
10.	3 + 3 = 6	**35.**	8 + 4 = 12
11.	7 + 7 = 14	**36.**	10 + 7 = 17
12.	9 + 3 = 12	**37.**	10 + 1 = 11
13.	8 + 6 = 14	**38.**	5 + 3 = 8
14.	6 + 5 = 11	**39.**	3 + 2 = 5
15.	8 + 2 = 10	**40.**	2 + 1 = 3
16.	7 +1 = 8	**41.**	7 + 3 = 10
17.	7 + 1 = 8	**42.**	9 + 6 = 15
18.	4 + 3 = 7	**43.**	4 + 4 = 8
19.	7 + 4 = 11	**44.**	6 + 6 = 12
20.	4 + 2 = 6	**45.**	9 + 7 = 16
21.	8 + 7 = 15	**46.**	8 + 5 = 13
22.	6 + 4 = 10	**47.**	8 + 1 = 9
23.	0 + 1 = 1	**48.**	10 + 2 = 12
24.	10 + 10 = 20	**49.**	4 + 1 = 5
25.	7 + 5 = 12	**50.**	6 + 2 = 8

Math Facts, page 65

51.	10 - 9 = 1	**76.**	8 - 2 = 6
52.	12 - 1 = 11	**77.**	11 - 5 = 6
53.	7 - 2 = 5	**78.**	18 - 9 = 9
54.	10 - 3 = 7	**79.**	10 - 8 = 2
55.	5 - 1 = 4	**80.**	15 - 8 = 7
56.	7 - 1 = 6	**81.**	9 - 5 = 4
57.	9 - 2 = 7	**82.**	10 - 7 = 3
58.	12 - 4 = 8	**83.**	4 - 2 = 2
59.	12 - 5 = 7	**84.**	8 - 3 = 5
60.	4 - 3 = 1	**85.**	5 - 4 = 1
61.	14 - 9 = 5	**86.**	9 - 3 = 6
62.	9 - 8 = 1	**87.**	9 - 7 = 2
63.	9 - 4 = 5	**88.**	20 - 10 = 10
64.	12 - 6 = 6	**89.**	6 - 3 = 3
65.	8 - 4 = 4	**90.**	9 - 9 = 0
66.	6 - 4 = 2	**91.**	3 - 1 = 2
67.	8 - 6 = 2	**92.**	10 - 5 = 5
68.	8 - 1 = 7	**93.**	11 - 9 = 2
69.	10 - 2 = 8	**94.**	7 - 6 = 1
70.	8 - 7 = 1	**95.**	10 - 4 = 6
71.	13 - 6 = 7	**96.**	7 - 3 = 4
72.	16 - 8 = 8	**97.**	8 - 5 = 3
73.	7 - 5 = 2	**98.**	10 - 8 = 2
74.	9 - 6 = 3	**99.**	1 - 0 = 1
75.	7 - 4 = 3	**100.**	9 - 1 = 8

100th Day Joke Fun, page 66

What do get when you cross a centipede with a parrot? Answer: A Walkie Talkie!

100th Day Joke Fun, page 67

What has 50 legs, but can't walk? Answer: Half of a centipede!